The
Leadership Engine

Building Leaders at Every Level

By Noel Tichy
with Eli Cohen

Introduction

**By Price Pritchett,
Chairman of Pritchett Rummler-Brache**

For more than 25 years, I've consulted to senior executives in some of the world's largest corporations, helping them tackle tough business issues around change, growth and innovation. We've worked with our clients through gut-wrenching mergers, painful downsizings and stressful growth spurts. Time and time again, those experiences have confirmed just how crucial strong leadership is during destabilized, challenging situations.

People, by nature, prefer to work with and for strong leaders. We particularly long for high-quality leadership during times of uncertainty, ambiguity and change. Given today's relentless and ever-accelerating rate of change — and with a future that looks so vague and challenging — leadership ability is a more precious asset to the organization than ever before.

As the labor market has tightened significantly over the past few years, the demand for talent has reached new highs. Organizations are competing for leaders the same way sports teams or Hollywood studios compete for marquee talent. People who can lead carry a premium. Problem is, many companies can't ante up to compete in the open market for this talent. Even those who can afford to play this high-stakes game are asking themselves if "buying rather than building" is the best long-term solution. For all these reasons, leadership development ranks high on the agenda for most organizations.

In looking at our portfolio of offerings, we came to the conclusion that Pritchett Rummler-Brache should add leadership training to our list of core competencies. We conducted an exhaustive search for an alliance on this topic. We wanted to establish a long-term relationship with a partner whose messages and business philosophies complement ours. More importantly, we wanted to align ourselves with someone who could add significant value for our clients.

Of all the leadership experts we considered, we selected Noel Tichy, who recently authored an excellent book called *The Leadership Engine: How Winning Companies Build Leaders at Every Level* (HarperBusiness 1997), which was named one of *BusinessWeek* magazine's Ten Best Business Books of 1997. We chose to partner with Noel and his associates because of his outstanding reputation and our shared beliefs that —

- Leadership and change are inseparable
- Leaders have a personal responsibility to develop other leaders
- Success depends upon leaders at every level of the organization facing reality and doing what works

Knowing that time is your most precious resource, we've condensed Noel Tichy and Eli Cohen's best-selling book, *The Leadership Engine*, down to this rapid-read handbook in order to introduce the major concepts in less than an hour of reading time. This handbook isn't designed to replace *The Leadership Engine*. The rich stories and detailed accounts of leaders profiled in *The Leadership Engine* cannot, and should not, be condensed. However, we "faced reality" and acknowledged that many people might never be exposed to *The Leadership Engine* without a preview of its contents. We're convinced that reading this handbook will encourage those wanting to develop their leadership competency to read *The Leadership Engine* from cover to cover. There are no shortcuts to leadership, and this handbook won't be enough to see you through. However, it is a beginning point. And it's a good first step toward becoming the leader you potentially can be.

In addition, we've put together a dynamic one-day Coaches' Clinic called *The Leadership Engine: Building Leaders at Every Level*. Noel worked with us to design this eight-hour, information-rich experience that's packed with interactive exercises, powerful videos and relevant business benchmarking. We see this clinic as an essential second step in your leadership development plan.

Our goal? To help you personally meet the growing leadership needs of your organization. As new technologies enable new organizational structures and different work approaches, power is being redistributed. This changes the way we conduct business. It means leadership must become more local. Larger numbers of people must become capable of leading, simply because they are operating with more power, more information and more decision-making authority than before. *The Leadership Engine* can help you play a part in this migration of leadership ability across your organization.

*"All people have untapped
leadership potential,
just as all people have untapped
athletic potential.
With coaching and practice,
we can all get much better at it."*

— Noel M. Tichy, author of *The Leadership Engine*

Table of Contents

PART ONE: WINNING LEADERS ARE TEACHING LEADERS

*"At the end of the day you bet on people,
not strategies."*

— Larry Bossidy, CEO, AlliedSignal

Chapter One:
Leaders Developing Leaders

"The scarcest resource in the world today is leadership talent capable of continuously transforming organizations to win in tomorrow's world."

— Noel M. Tichy, author of *The Leadership Engine*

If you show up on the right day every couple of weeks at GE's Crotonville leadership development institute, you will find Jack Welch, CEO of GE, teaching. Welch spends an enormous amount of time giving speeches to employees and taking the hot seat in question-and-answer sessions, but he also teaches interactively. He has a variety of modules, usually half a day at a time, that he uses to teach leadership. In the most senior program, he asks, among other things, "If you were named CEO of GE tomorrow, what would you do?" Welch uses the question to orchestrate a no-holds-barred discussion in which he jousts with participants and hones their analytic abilities and leadership instincts by having them also joust with each other. He considers such sessions essential and is proud of his commitment. Says Welch, "I've gone to Crotonville every two weeks for 17 years to interact with new employees, middle managers and senior managers. I have not missed a session."

In an 18-month period shortly before he became CEO of PepsiCo in early 1996, Roger Enrico spent nearly a third of his time at his houses in the Cayman Islands and Montana. This may seem like a pretty unusual way for the vice chairman of a multi-billion dollar company based in Purchase, New York, to do his job. But his job is exactly what Roger Enrico was doing. And he was doing it extremely well. In these remote off-site settings, away from the daily demands of making potato chips, selling sodas and resolving assorted day-to-day problems, Enrico was preparing PepsiCo to survive and thrive into the 21st Century. He was running his own personal "war college" to develop a new generation of leaders for PepsiCo. At the end of the 18 months, Enrico had prepared 100 leaders as Pepsi's next generation. And he had fostered some of their best ideas, resulting in an estimated $2 billion in top-line growth.

In Santa Clara, California, Andy Grove goes into the classroom several times a year to teach Intel managers how to lead in an industry in which the product (microprocessors) doubles in capacity every 18 months. In Grove's teaching sessions, he discusses the role of leaders in detecting and navigating the turbulent industry shifts that many companies fail to survive. Why does Grove take the time to do this? Because he believes that having leaders at all levels of Intel who can spot the trends and who have the courage to act will enable Intel to prosper while competitors falter. So Grove is dedicated to teaching and developing others at all levels to be winning leaders.

Recently in Coronado, California, Rear Admiral Ray Smith, a Navy SEAL since the Vietnam War, visited a class of SEALs graduating from Basic Underwater Demolition SEAL training. Only 20% of the candidates who enter this elite six-month program survive its great physical and mental demands to graduate. Throughout the day, Smith, in his fifties, participated in the same physical training as the SEAL candidates who were all in their twenties. At the end of the day, he met alone with the graduates. Speaking as a successful leader who had been exactly where they were, he laid out for them personally his teachable point of view on the leadership duties of becoming a SEAL, the conduct, honor and teamwork required, and the need for them to develop other leaders.

These four leaders represent the Olympians. During their early lives, they built up excellent track records. Then they took on the next challenge — becoming great teachers who could develop other leaders.

Are you ready for the challenge? The rest of this rapid-read handbook will give you some of the why, what and how of becoming a better leader and engendering those same traits in others.

Exercise:

Imagine that Tom Brokaw is standing in front of you with a microphone. He's doing a special on world-class leaders. You've just been asked to tell 40 million viewers your point of view on what makes a great leader, and how you embody these principles. What would you say?

Chapter Two:
Winning Organizations Are Teaching Organizations

"How are you doing as a leader? The answer is how are the people you lead doing? Do they learn? Do they visit customers? Do they manage conflict? Do they initiate change? Are they growing and getting promoted? You won't remember when you retire what you did in the first quarter or the third. What you'll remember is how many people you developed — how many people you helped have a better career because of your interest and your dedication to their development. When confused as to how you're doing as a leader, find out how the people you lead are doing. You'll know the answer."

— Larry Bossidy, CEO, AlliedSignal

In my 25 years as an organizational psychologist and management consultant, I have seen lots of troubled companies up close, from the inside. I have also worked with a number of winning companies such as General Electric, where I worked full-time as head of GE's Crotonville leadership development institute. A major part of my job has always been figuring out what works and what doesn't. Several years ago, however, the great disparity between the track records of the corporate winners and losers prompted me to step back and to tackle the broader question: Why do some companies succeed while others fail?

The answer I have come up with is that winning companies win because they have good leaders who nurture the development of other leaders at all levels of the organization. The ultimate test of success for an organization is not whether it can win today, but whether it can keep winning tomorrow and the day after.

Therefore, the ultimate test for a leader is not whether he or she can make smart decisions and take decisive action, but whether he or she can teach others to be leaders and build an organization that remains successful even when he or she is not around. The key ability of winning organizations and winning leaders is creating leaders.

Exercise:

1. Write down the name of a person who taught you something about leadership. It's not essential that you had a formal reporting relationship to this person. The relationship might have been personal or professional.

2. What leadership principle(s) did you learn from this person?

3. What have you purposefully done to teach others your beliefs about leadership?

Chapter Three:
Two Criteria of
Winning Companies

*"Our dream is to shape a global enterprise with the reach and resources
of a big company — the body of a big company — but the thirst to
learn, the compulsion to share and the bias for action — the soul —
of a small company."*

— Jack Welch, CEO, General Electric

*There is only one surviving component of the original members
of the Dow Jones Industrial Average.*

Let me define what I mean by "winning" when I talk about winning
companies. I have just two criteria:

1. **Success in adding value.** There are many ways you could choose to
   measure this, but for corporations, I don't think there's a better one
   than the capital markets. For not-for-profit organizations, the test is
   whether they are growing and improving their use of assets
   (productivity).

2. **Sustained excellence.** For established companies to qualify as
   winners, they must have a continuing track record of success in the
   capital markets. A quarter or two in the limelight as a "darling of
   Wall Street" doesn't do it. The test for non-profits is: Do they have
   a continuing impact, and are they growing to impact more people?

The companies that consistently win — the Intels, the Compaqs, the ServiceMasters of the world — don't just have one strong leader or just a few at the top. They have lots of strong leaders, and they have them at all levels of the organization. In the time it takes for a question to be passed up the ladder and a decision to be handed back down, the customer will have gone somewhere else or the opportunity will have been missed. It takes leaders at all levels to achieve the speed a company needs to survive.

This requires an organization that isn't just built to last, but one that is *built to change*. In the future, the real core competence of companies will be the ability to destroy and remake themselves continuously and creatively to meet customer demands.

Exercise:

1. What is your company's average return to shareholders over the last three years? Over the last five years? What about your competitors?

2. What are the implications of this for moving your career forward?

Chapter Four:
Leadership Means Mastering Revolutionary Change

"Senior managers got to where they are by having been good at what they do...so it's not surprising that they will keep implementing the same strategic and tactical moves that worked for them during the course of their careers...I call this phenomenon the inertia of success. It is extremely dangerous."

— Andy Grove, Chairman, Intel

Becoming a world-class leader requires the ability to master revolutionary change. It requires taking on the dramatic challenge of creatively destroying and remaking organizations in order to improve them. Not just once, but repeatedly. In order for organizations to win, revolutions, driven by leaders with ideas and the heart and guts to bring them alive, must become a way of life.

There is no doubt that revolutionary change can be painful. But in all facets of life, including business, one must master change. Faced with increasingly difficult, large and frequent shifts in economies, societies and marketplaces, organizations need leaders who can redirect life's emotional energies.

Leaders of any institution, private or public, must be willing repeatedly to let go of old ideas and old ways of doing things and to develop new and better ones. And they must be able to help each and every employee generate the high level of positive energy needed to do the same.

The only thing that never changes is the fact that everything changes, and building a Leadership Engine is about creating organizations and developing leaders who survive and thrive through change.

Exercise:

1. What changes are you and your organization currently facing?

_____

_____

_____

2. What are some likely consequences of failing to adapt to these changes?

_____

_____

_____

Chapter Five:
Leaders Stage Revolutions

"First, you never announce that you're launching a change agenda. The reason is simple: change agendas have been done to death in most companies. My first two days on the job at U S WEST I found out all the programs of the month that they'd had in the last four years. If you come in and announce, 'Here's the next change program,' you're dead. You just painted a target on your chest.

Instead you do several very high-impact things in the first 30 days that are immediately distinguishable and immediately shake up the organization. I thought U S WEST was standing on a burning platform. Unfortunately a lot of people didn't see it that way. So I had a 30-day agenda to create a buzz in the organization to demonstrate that something was different.

For example, service was in the tank. So on my second day on the job, I initiated a scheduled phone call for my department heads to review service performance in all 14 states. I scheduled that call for 6 a.m. I told my department heads, 'You're going to service the customer between 8 a.m. and 5 p.m., so the call happens at 6 a.m.' Having to get your butt up at 6 a.m. to understand where your business is, that's a watershed event for an organization that's asleep."

— Bob Knowling, Executive Vice President of Operations
   and Technology, U S WEST Communications

Within 18 months, Bob Knowling took the 20,000-person network organization at U S WEST and turned it around. Rather than being over budget by hundreds of millions of dollars, it was under budget.

Rather than being sued by customers and offering the worst service in its industry, it was at the middle of the pack and moving up.

In a broad sense, leaders are revolutionaries. They are constantly challenging the status quo and looking around to see if they are doing the right things, or if those things can be done better or smarter. And most importantly, when they spot something that needs to be changed, they do something about it. In more concrete terms, leaders do two specific things:

- **See reality.** They size up the current situation as it really is, not as it used to be or as they would like it to be.
- **Take action.** They mobilize the appropriate responses.

This is a lot harder than it sounds. Seeing reality requires that leaders remove the filters that screen out the things they might not want to see, acknowledge their own shortcomings and their companies', and accept the need for change. Facing reality is about personally accepting the case for change. This is often referred to as "acknowledging the burning platform."

Some companies can't do it. In retailing, Sears and JC Penney accepted their lot in life and assumed that there was little growth to be achieved in being a merchandiser. Meanwhile, Sam Walton drove around in a beat-up pickup truck, realizing that there was a huge customer base in small towns across the country that was being ignored. His response was to create Wal-Mart, a company that revolutionized the concept of the general merchandiser and is now bigger than both Sears and JC Penney.

In established businesses, seeing reality is often more difficult because it means letting go of ingrained ways of thinking and working. But the best do it. At GE, when Jack Welch took over, there was the "GE Way," perfected over decades and hailed as the most sophisticated way to manage a big company. Welch thought this asset was actually the company's greatest liability. He threw out the playbook and surrounded himself with others who saw the same reality: that companies as slow as GE couldn't survive in the global marketplace. They set about shutting and selling some businesses, buying others and giving people in the company the freedom to act quickly and decisively. GE is now the world's most valuable company.

Facing reality is the first crucial step that leaders must take if their organizations are going to respond appropriately. But it is just the starting point. Once a leader has figured out what the problem is, whether it's a challenge or an opportunity, he or she has to decide on a response, determine what actions need to be taken and make sure those actions get implemented promptly and well.

Implementation of a massive organizational change is the hardest part, because it requires selling the new response (including the case for change) and weeding out the resisters and the superfluous work. Implementation of an idea requires values, emotional energy and the edge (or guts) to see it through to the end.

Just as the word implies, leaders accomplish things by leading. That is, by guiding and motivating other people. Dictators issue orders, using fear and punishment to command compliance. Leaders shape people's opinions and win their enthusiasm, using every available opportunity to send out their message and win supporters.

Exercise:

1. What are the strategic actions you need to take to respond to new realities?

2. How much resistance do you expect to face? How will you deal with it?

Chapter Six:
Four Steps for Building Leaders at Every Level

"The legacy I want to leave is helping people understand that sometimes it's really good if people aren't like you. There are different packages that work, and different styles that work. And not that it's just OK to be different...sometimes it's better."

— Debra Dunn, General Manager of Test and Measurement,
Hewlett-Packard

Winning organizations and people who build leaders at every level come in all shapes, sizes and nationalities, and can be found in any industry. The goods and services they produce and the strategies and tactics they employ are widely divergent. But they all share a set of fundamental similarities.

- First, leaders with a proven track record of success take direct responsibility for the development of other leaders.

- Second, leaders who develop other leaders have teachable points of view in the specific areas of ideas, values and something that I call E^3 — emotional energy and edge. Winning leaders and teachers have ideas that they can articulate and teach to others about both how to make the organization successful in the marketplace and how to develop other leaders.

- Third, leaders embody their teachable points of view in living stories. They tell stories about their pasts that explain their learning experiences and their beliefs. And they create stories about the future of their organizations that engage others both emotionally and intellectually to attain the winning future that they describe.

• Finally, because winning leaders invest a considerable amount of time in developing other leaders, they have well-defined methodologies and thoroughly developed coaching and teaching techniques. Among these is a willingness to admit mistakes and show vulnerability in order to serve as effective role models for others.

"Every person in a key position has to see himself or herself as a mini-CEO. They have to conceptualize what has to be done in the same way the CEO has. Then it cascades."

— Michael Walsh, former CEO, Tenneco

Exercise:

Take a moment to assess how ready you are to develop other leaders based on the following criteria. Circle the number that best describes your current leadership capabilities.

	Never		Sometimes		Always

1. *Focus*   1   2   3   4   5
   When coaching others, you focus on the total picture of leadership — both hard, analytic issues and soft issues such as how you energize people and how you make decisions.

2. *Teachable point of view*   1   2   3   4   5
   You have a clearly articulated point of view on the ideas, values, energy and edge required to be a winning leader in your company.

3. *Commitment*   1   2   3   4   5
   You personally see developing others as an important part of your leadership. Opportunities to develop other leaders are not limited to formal teaching programs.

4. *Role model*   1   2   3   4   5
   When you teach others, you are open to learning. You can readily name things that you learned from the people you are coaching. People feel comfortable in expressing their own viewpoints, debating them with you and coming out with a different perspective.

If you scored 5 on all of these, you are rating yourself an outstanding leader/teacher. Congratulations! If you scored lower than 5, I congratulate you as well. The first step in teaching others is an honest self-assessment of how prepared you are to do so. The rest of this handbook will be dedicated to improving your ability to develop others, no matter where you fell on the scales.

Chapter Seven:
All People Have Untapped Leadership Potential

"As leaders, we do not set the goals high enough for our people. Leadership is salesmanship. Getting people to say, 'C'mon, we can do this.'"

— Father William Cunningham, co-founder of Focus: HOPE

I have a very simple thesis: all people have untapped leadership potential, just as all people have untapped athletic potential. There are clear differences due to nature and nurture, that is, genes and development, as to how much untapped potential there may be. But no matter what level of athletic or leadership performance a person currently exhibits, he or she can make quantum improvements.

Not everyone can be the CEO of a multi-billion dollar corporation, just as not everyone can be an Olympian or win at Wimbledon, but with coaching and practice, we can all be a lot better than we are. The important teaching point is that leadership is there in you.

It's never too early or too late to take on the challenge of improving your leadership abilities and developing them in others. The scarcest resource in the world today is leadership talent capable of continuously transforming organizations to win in tomorrow's world. The individuals and organizations that build Leadership Engines and that invest in leaders developing other leaders have a sustainable competitive advantage.

Exercise:

1. At one time, in high school or college, at work, on an athletic team or in a community or church group, you made something happen through other people that would never have occurred without your leadership. Take a moment now to get a clear picture in your mind of a time in your life when you were most proud of yourself as a leader. Write a brief description of that time on the lines below. Reflect on what made this leadership experience important to you.

_____

_____

_____

_____

_____

2. What characteristics of effective leadership did you demonstrate during this experience?

_____

_____

_____

_____

_____

PART TWO: BECOMING A TEACHER

"Somewhere along the way,
we either told people, or they surmised,
...that it was a paint-by-the-numbers system.
That if you use these tools in
this sequence in this way, success is inevitable...
[If it were that easy]
I wouldn't need a manager, I'd have a machine."

— Roger Enrico, CEO, PepsiCo

Chapter Eight:
Leaders Are Teachers

"The basis of leadership is the capacity of the leader to change the mindset, the framework of another person."

— Warren Bennis, Distinguished Professor of Business Administration,
University of Southern California

It's possible to build an organization that succeeds, at least for a while, without developing leadership in others. Autocrats have produced a winner or two. People who are great individual contributors can sometimes get their organizations by with the force of their own personality or intelligence. But the companies that win most often are the ones whose leaders invest the time and energy to develop lots of leaders.

One of my favorite examples is Michael Jordan. In the book *Sacred Hoops*, Coach Phil Jackson talks about his work with Jordan. With such a gifted athlete, no coach could do much to improve his basketball play. So Jackson focused his efforts with Jordan on making the superstar a true leader of the team. And it worked. In 1989, five years after joining the league and the same year that Jackson became head coach of the Bulls, Jordan began to see his role not just as stealing balls and scoring points, but as a leader whose job also was to help raise the level of play of every other player on the team. It is this contribution, Jordan's ability to help his teammates be better players, more than his superb athletic talent, that has made the Chicago Bulls the world's winningest basketball team.

Like athletic teams with lots of strong players, companies with lots of leaders not only compete better today, but they are better prepared to repeat the performance tomorrow.

Teaching others to be leaders requires that a leader have two things:

• **A serious commitment to teaching** — which means that they make it a top priority in everything they do.

• **Teachable points of view**

Winning leaders spend a lot of their time teaching. Sometimes it's in formal settings, like a workshop or a training session. But if you watch them, you will note that they are always teaching, even when they appear to be doing something else. Leaders treat every face-to-face encounter as a teaching and learning opportunity.

This section of this rapid-read handbook will help you develop your own teachable points of view.

Chapter Nine:
Developing a Teachable Point of View

"A point of view is worth 50 IQ points."

— Roger Enrico, CEO, PepsiCo

Having a teachable point of view is what allows leaders to be effective teachers. We all know that good athletes don't always make good coaches because it's one thing to be able to do something, and quite another to be able to explain it. Great leaders are great teachers because they not only know how to do many things, but they also organize their thoughts so that they can help others learn to do them. In other words, they not only have points of view about how the world operates and how to get things done, but have also invested the time and the effort to make those points of view "teachable" to others.

To develop teachable points of view, leaders think about their experiences, draw lessons from what they know and then figure out how to share those lessons with others. Most people have teachable points of view about simple things. We not only save important documents on our computer's hard drive, but we can explain the "why" and "how" of file storage. Winning leaders, however, have teachable points of view on a broad range of less tangible and more complicated topics.

Leadership is more about thinking, judging, acting and motivating than about strategies, methodologies and tools. Therefore, good leaders develop teachable points of view that help others learn to think, judge, act and motivate.

Simply put, if you're not teaching, you're not leading. If you want to become a teacher, the best place to start is by developing your own teachable points of view about: ideas, values, emotional energy and edge.

Chapter Ten:
The Heart of Leadership —
It Starts With Ideas

"A company beset by malaise and steady deterioration suffers from something far more serious than inefficiencies.
Its business [ideas] have become obsolete."

— Peter Drucker

Let me tell you a couple of stories:

1) Roberto Goizueta, the former Chairman of Coca-Cola, asked a question of his senior managers:
>   *"What is our market share?"*
>   *"45%," came the confident reply.*
>   *"How many ounces of liquid does a human being need to drink a day?" Goizueta asked.*
>   *"64 ounces a day," came the puzzled reply.*
>   *"On average, how many ounces of all of our products does a person drink per day?" Goizueta asked.*
>   *"2 ounces," came their response.*
>   *"What's our market share?" came his final query.*
With that one big idea, Roberto Goizueta changed the future of a 100-year-old institution. Coca-Cola managers had assumed that traditional soft drink markets were saturated. They had assumed that the company couldn't grow rapidly, and that any growth it could get would come from buying other businesses like shrimp farming or movie studios. With one big idea, that the competition was not PepsiCo, but was in fact any other beverage, Goizueta put Coca-Cola managers on the search for growth opportunities everywhere in the world. Today Coca-Cola is one of the most valuable companies on earth because of this.

2) "The PC isn't really a computational device. It's really a communications device."

Bob Stearns, the head of strategy at Compaq Computer, uttered these words in early 1996 as the impact of the Internet was just becoming apparent. Since then, he and Eckhard Pfeiffer, the company's CEO, have completely changed Compaq from a company based on the personal computer to one that can offer a full range of products and services for computing and communicating. This one idea has changed the direction of Compaq and nearly doubled its size in two years.

The point of these stories is that leaders have ideas. They have a strategy, or "central business idea," and they have ideas about how to carry out that strategy. A company's central business idea explains why it is in business and how it is going to make money. If a company is going to win against its competitors, everyone in the organization must know what they are aiming to achieve.

Most companies start out with a good "central idea." Otherwise, they would never have gotten up and running. But along the way, many companies lose their focus. Or they achieve their initial goal, like NASA after it put a man on the moon, and don't come up with a new one. One of the jobs of a leader is to make sure that a company has a good central business idea, and that everyone knows what it is.

Because circumstances change, a business idea that was good yesterday may not be so good today. When that happens, leaders must change the idea, and then get everyone in the company working to achieve the new idea.

To get its central idea carried out, an organization needs leaders at all levels to develop ideas about implementation. So it's essential that they, and everyone in the organization, completely understand the central idea.

Some leaders excel at coming up with ideas. But you don't have to be an "idea person" to be a good leader. Lew Platt, the head of Hewlett-Packard, describes himself as "not an idea person." He is good at recognizing good ideas, however, so he surrounds himself with people who come up with lots of ideas. Then he picks out the best ones.

The important thing isn't that a leader come up with good, clear ideas but that he or she makes sure that the company has them…and that everyone knows what those ideas are.

To keep an organization focused on good ideas, a leader must do two things:

- **Develop ideas**
- **Communicate those ideas clearly**

Exercise:

1. What are the big ideas your company was built on?

_____

_____

_____

_____

2. Have competitors come up with new ideas that are threatening you?

_____

_____

_____

_____

3. Where will your new ideas come from?

_____

_____

_____

_____

Chapter Eleven:
Values for Winning

*"In the 1980s, I would be managing six or seven people.
Today I manage 15, and it's on its way to 20."*

— Manufacturing Manager, GE Appliances, Louisville, KY.

There's an old saying that people talk about having good values so that they won't have to live by them. But for winning leaders and their companies, that's not the case.

That's because managers like the one from GE above are finding that they now have to behave very differently from the way they did just a few years ago. When you can't control, dictate or monitor (and you can't do that for 20 people at a time), the only thing you *can* do is trust. This means that you let people make their own decisions. And you have to have a common set of values to make sure that those decisions are ones that will move the company ahead and ones that will make you proud.

Clear ideas help people to act quickly and independently by giving them a shared vision of what they are trying to accomplish. Values provide a similar shared understanding by addressing the "how." How do people in the company work together — what does "teamwork" mean? How open are people to feedback from customers and each other? How much does a company value experimentation versus stability? How does it weigh the value of teamwork against individual initiative?

When a company has clear ideas and clear values, people can figure out what to do without having to ask for guidance. Most people understand that the right strategies and ideas can give a company a competitive advantage. But good leaders realize that the right values can make a difference as well.

There are some big values, like honesty, integrity and the sanctity of an agreement, that never change. But others can and should change to support changing business ideas. When Jack Welch took over GE, the company had values of stability and respect for authority which supported its business idea: to be a centrally-controlled, industrial company. Welch's new ideas were to take GE into unpredictable new markets and to give people more autonomy. So he created values such as speed and self-confidence to help people survive in these new environments.

It's the job of a leader to make sure that a company's values support its central business idea.

Exercise:

1. Write down the values of your organization — not as they are printed on the placard on the wall — but as you see them lived on a daily basis.

2. Explain how these values support the current business ideas.

3. Are any of these values getting in the way of new business ideas?

Chapter Twelve:
Speaking With Words and Actions

In 1982, James E. Burke, the head of Johnson & Johnson, got the most important call of his life. Seven people in Chicago had died when they took Tylenol pills that had been laced with poison. Over the next few days, government officials and Johnson & Johnson executives scrambled to figure out what was happening. For Johnson & Johnson, this was a crucible — the whole world was watching.

Within days it was proved that this was an isolated incident and that J&J was the victim of a terrible crime. In spite of its innocence, J&J continued removing 31 million bottles from store shelves and taking returns from customers. The decision cost the company $100 million.

This unflinching show of concern for customers led to an almost immediate recovery in Tylenol sales. How did the company react so quickly and with such integrity to its biggest crisis in history?

"We had hundreds of people making decisions all the time during the Tylenol incident," says Burke. These people are the ones who saved the company and they did it because they knew the first line of the company's Credo — "We believe our first responsibility is to the doctors, nurses and patients, to mothers and fathers and all others who use our products and services..."

At Johnson & Johnson, the Credo is the cornerstone of a values system that works because leaders take it seriously. Like other values-driven companies, leaders at Johnson & Johnson do the following five things to make sure that their organizations understand and live by the values:

- Clearly articulate a set of values

- Continually reflect on the values to make sure they're appropriate to achieving the desired goals

- Embody the values with their own behavior

- Encourage others to apply the values in their own decisions and actions

- Aggressively confront and deal with pockets of ignorance and resistance

Whether they want to or not, leaders set the tone and determine the values of a company. Good leaders, therefore, are very careful to make sure that everything they do — from designing compensation systems to setting customer service practices — reflects the values they want the company to have.

Winning leaders outshine the losers because they back up words with actions, embody their values and wrestle daily with their application.

To help people really understand what living up to their values means, leaders don't just hand out a list and command compliance. Rather, they encourage people to examine their values and consider how they play out in day-to-day situations. It's one thing to know that you think teamwork is important, but the test is: are you a good team player? Do you reward the people who are cooperative? And do you fire the ones who are self-serving?

Exercise:

1. What are some tough decisions that tested your values? What
   did your decision show about how well you live up to your
   stated values?

2. How are you teaching people about values before tough decisions
   arise?

Chapter Thirteen:
Making It Happen —
Getting Energy Out of Everyone

"At the end of the day, I feel, every single person has got to come away from a meeting with me with something positive...My goal is that at every single session, people feel they've gained something from the experience."

— Carlos Cantu, CEO, ServiceMaster

Good leaders pay attention to creating positive energy the same way they pay attention to spreading ideas and teaching values. That's because they know that positive energy helps people overcome obstacles and rise to new challenges. They also know that a leader is never "energy-neutral." You are either giving people energy or you are sapping it from them.

One way that leaders create positive energy in others is by exhibiting positive energy themselves. They work hard, with a determination that shows that they really care about the goal the organization is trying to accomplish. Phil Myers is a ServiceMaster account manager who works in the Chicago area. When I interviewed him, he asked me to wear running shoes to the interview so that I could follow him as he raced around the hospital for which he is responsible.

While leaders never tire, they never use their energy to intimidate. Their enthusiasm is almost a magnetic force, bringing people toward them. They engage other people to join them by making them see that their contributions can make a difference. Winning leaders do this in a number of ways, including coaching people, advising them and listening to their input. They also show respect for others by not wasting their time with meetings that ramble on and don't produce results.

Exercise:

1. What are you doing to keep yourself energized?

_____

_____

_____

2. When was a time that you generated positive energy in a situation? What effect did this have on the outcome?

_____

_____

_____

Chapter Fourteen:
Capitalizing on Change

One day in April, 1992, at 6:00 a.m., a young manager named Tom Tiller herded forty manufacturing workers aboard a bus at General Electric's range-building plant at Appliance Park in Louisville, Kentucky. They headed for the annual Kitchen and Bath Show in Atlanta. They were setting out on a crucial reconnaissance mission. Appliance Park, a sprawling 1,100-acre complex, had once employed more than 23,000 workers. By 1992, the company had closed down several of its production lines and employment was down to 9,000. The range line was losing $10 million a year and the jobs of everyone on that bus were in jeopardy.

GE hadn't produced a new set of kitchen ranges in 20 years. On the bus ride, the forty people from different departments got to know each other and got comfortable together. At the show in Atlanta they went through every product and decided what ideas they wanted to use. At the end of the trip, there was a very clear sense that "We've got to do something. We've got to do it fast. We don't have 142 years to do it, and we're going to be the ones to get it done." And they did.

Within 18 months, the people on the bus had spearheaded an effort that had three new products designed, built and delivered to the market. The plant went from a $10 million loss to a $35 million profit in 1994.

One of the most remarkable things about winning organizations is how often they manage to come out of times of trouble even stronger than they were before the problems arose. The reason for this is that stress always produces energy in people. It's a fact of nature, and winning leaders are masters at channeling that energy away from the usual complaining, infighting and resistance, and harnessing it for productive uses.

Leaders enlist the people affected by a challenge or difficulty in taking the initiative and responsibility for overcoming it. This almost always produces not only positive energy, but also positive results. And these results often go beyond just solving the immediate problem. That's because in joining together and working their way out of trouble, everyone in the organization gets energized. They also learn how to think and work more effectively.

In order to get people energized to attack problems, leaders work to make sure that five conditions exist:

1. **A sense of urgency.** Leaders focus people on the fact that there is a real problem and that it isn't going to go away unless they do something.

2. **A mission worth achieving.** Change can be frightening, so it's not enough for people to understand that they can't keep doing things the old way. Leaders have to help them envision a specific future that looks a lot better.

3. **Goals that stretch people's abilities.** Stretch goals must be high enough to inspire extraordinary effort, but they can't appear so unreasonable or unattainable that they discourage people from reaching for them.

4. **A spirit of teamwork.** People need to feel that "We're all in this together." The risks seem less risky and goals seem more achievable when you are part of a team. Leaders make sure that people know that the leader is on the team with them.

5. **A realistic expectation that the team can succeed.** Leaders build people's confidence by making sure that all parts of a problem are addressed, so that if people do their part, the solution will work.

Also, while leaders do use times of difficulty to create positive energy, they don't just sit around and wait for problems to create a crisis. If there is no immediately pressing difficulty, they often stir things up. They break down tired, old bureaucracies or they set new stretch goals and challenge people to meet them.

Winning companies stay ahead because their people have lots of energy and they use it wisely. Leaders who pay attention to creating positive energy almost always get positive results.

Exercise:

1. What are some changes taking place that are causing negative energy (fear, paranoia, panic, confusion) in your company?

2. How is this negative energy hurting performance?

3. What are some things you can do to turn the negative energy into positive energy?

Chapter Fifteen:
Edge — The Courage to See Reality and Act on It

"The best way to get people to accept the need for change is not to give them a choice. The organization has to know that there is a leader at the top who has made up his mind, that he is surrounded by leaders who have made up their minds, and that they're going to drive forward no matter what."

— Bill Weiss, Retired Chairman and CEO, Ameritech

Leaders who have *edge* have an unflinching readiness to face reality and the courage to act. Bill Weiss displayed it when he started a revolution at Ameritech in the early 1990s. While the 65,000-person company appeared to be going along just fine, Weiss knew it had to get ready for a different future. So he unequivocally launched the company on its path to transformation. For three years he personally embodied that transformation by spending hundreds of days on issues of changing the company's structure and culture. He did this by passing over his heirs apparent and picking young aggressive change agents to lead the next generation. In that time, Ameritech completely changed its structure, started several high-growth businesses and developed a new culture to support its strategy.

Edge decisions may not be pleasant or popular in the short term. But a great leader has the willingness to do things that will make the organization better, even though they may be scary or painful. And great leaders are unwilling to let the difficulty of the decision cloud what they know is the right thing to do.

Great leaders have edge in all their decisions. They make tough decisions about how to invest time, money and resources. Leaders demonstrate it when taking on new projects or discarding old ones in the face of resistance. Decisions to invest in a new business are often scary because they mean entering uncharted territory. Decisions to leave a business are often painful because people frequently lose their jobs. The common denominator is that they both require courage.

Leaders also make tough decisions about dealing with individuals. Edge requires giving people honest feedback — to help them improve. And it means confronting people who perform well but are abusive to others.

As unpleasant as these edge-ful decisions can be, people want their leaders to be decisive. Leaders can win others over by acting with a constant compass, teaching them why they reached their decisions and helping them develop their own edge.

The best way to teach edge is to put people in progressively more difficult situations where they have to make decisions, and then to give them feedback and support. Good leaders make it a policy that mistakes are coaching opportunities rather than causes for punishment.

Exercise:

1. What tough issues are you facing?

_____

_____

_____

2. What is holding you back?

_____

_____

_____

3. What is the effect of your delay?

_____

_____

_____

PART THREE: LEADING INTO THE FUTURE

*"The classic business story is much like the classic human story.
There is rise and fall, the overcoming of great odds,
the upholding of principles despite the cost, questions,
rivalry and succession, and even
the possibility of descent into madness."*

— Mark Helprin, author and member of the Board of Editors at
The Wall Street Journal

Chapter Sixteen:
Tying It All Together

"In speaking of stories, rather than messages or themes...leaders present a dynamic perspective to their followers: not just a headline or snapshot, but a drama that unfolds over time, in which they — the leaders and followers — are the principal characters or heroes."

— Howard Gardner, author of Leading Minds

Lots of executives have visions of how they want their company to be different in the future. They write about them in their annual reports to investors, and they plaster them on the cafeteria walls for employees to see. These visions are important because they define a concrete future for which everyone can aim. But by themselves, they aren't enough to make a company a winner.

In order to build a new future, people have to be willing to change things. Furthermore, they need to know what things to change and how to change them. In other words, they need motivation and a plan of attack. Winning leaders provide these by weaving their teachable points of view into stories.

One reason that people don't like to change is that change can be frightening. It means that they have to let go of things that are familiar and move into unknown territory. Even if they don't particularly like where they are, it's still hard to venture into the unknown. So leaders create stories about the future to take them there in their imaginations first, in order to let them see what it will be like to live in the new world.

Exercise:

1. Is your current business story compelling enough to inspire people?

2. How might that story need to change to ensure a successful future?

Chapter Seventeen:
Writing Your Leadership Story

"General Electric will be the world's most exciting enterprise. Where ideas win. Where people flourish and grow. Where the excitement of their work lives is transferred to their whole lives."

— Jack Welch, CEO, General Electric

The line above is from the future story that Jack Welch created to motivate people to help him build a "new GE." He had already laid out a business plan for how the company would compete and become the No. 1 or No. 2 company in each of its businesses. Now he was telling them what it would be like to work in that company. He was taking the abstract notion of corporate success and bringing it home to his listeners.

Another important element of "future stories" is that after exciting people with the prospect of a better future, they describe what individuals in the company will have to do to create that future. In the case of General Electric, Welch's stories told his people how they would have to tear down the walls that they had built between various parts of the company and start sharing ideas and helping each other. In the past, GE had been a hierarchical place where people would only work with people who were in their own units and at or near their level. To get to the future, Welch told them, they would have to forget about hierarchy and start thinking about the good of GE as a whole. He even coined a term for it; he called it "boundarylessness."

Some leaders seem to create stories that take people into the future instinctively. Others have to work at it.

But whether it's by instinct or conscious effort, good future stories always include three essential elements:

- The case for change — why we can't go on like we have been
- Where we are going — the picture of a better future
- How we will get there — the things that people as individuals will have to do, and stop doing, to create that future

I've said throughout this book that effective leaders have teachable points of view in the areas of:

- Teaching
- Learning
- Generating ideas
- Promoting values
- Creating energy
- Displaying edge

But these points of view can't be just dry intellectual concepts. To be effective, leaders have to bring them alive so that people can and will act on them. Stories are a powerful tool for doing just that.

Chapter Eighteen:
Leading Into the Future

"The role of the leader is all the more legitimate and powerful if top leaders help make their followers into leaders. Only by standing on their shoulders can true greatness in leadership be achieved."

— James MacGregor Burns, author and educator

In a very real sense, the future is what winning leadership is really all about. It is about building an organization that not only pleases customers and rewards shareholders today, but one that will also be able to do so again tomorrow and the next day.

Think of it as stewardship. The job of a leader is to take human capital, a company's most important asset, and to make it more valuable for the future. Good leaders do this by:

• **Sharing their sound business ideas and strong values.**

• **Developing teachable points of view. They show people how to generate their own ideas and values, and how to find the energy and edge to implement them.**

• **Engendering in others the desire and the ability to develop other people with ideas, values, energy and edge.**

In short, leaders teach. Teaching is not an occasional activity for them. It is at the heart of everything they do, day in and day out.

Nobody is a perfect leader. Leaders are human beings. So occasionally, they step in and do things themselves when it might be better to let someone else learn from the experience. They are not always instantly clear and totally articulate about what they are doing and why they are doing it. Sometimes they're even too nice and gentle to people in situations where exercising edge might be more appropriate. They all have their stronger and weaker points.

But all winning leaders understand the complex demands of their jobs and take all of them seriously. They have strong business ideas and operate their organizations according to deeply held values. They consciously build and channel the energy of their employees. They face reality and are willing to make tough decisions. And most importantly, they are conscientious learners and teachers, dedicated to developing everyone in their organizations to be learners and teachers as well.

The challenge to develop other leaders is daunting. It means thinking more, doing more and risking more. But in the end, it is the true test of leadership and the ultimate route to sustained winning. After preparing your teachable point of view, your story and your teaching methodologies, the question is: Will you do it?

Don't be too hard on yourself. Just keep working at it. Generate sound business ideas. Conduct yourself according to deeply held values. Build and channel your energy and the energy of those around you. Face reality with a willingness to make tough decisions. And above all, be a conscientious learner and teacher who develops others to be learners and teachers as well. That's how Leadership Engines are built. I wish you the best on this important journey.

Summary of Leadership Engine Concepts

Teachable Point of View

A teachable point of view is a leader's opinion about what it takes to
win in his or her business and what it takes to lead other people. In
order to teach others, leaders must develop their own teachable points of
view in four critical leadership areas: Ideas, Values, Emotional Energy
and Edge.

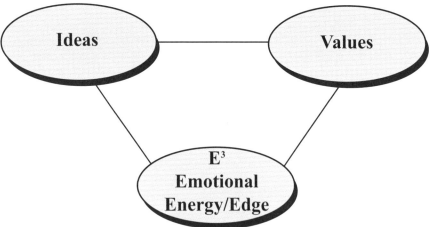

Ideas

A business starts with ideas about services or products in the
marketplace. Those ideas lead the business to produce and deliver value
to customers. For publicly traded companies, that value can ultimately
be linked to success in the capital markets. Leaders must be able to
explain to all stakeholders how the business succeeds in creating value.

Values

Winning organizations have leaders who can articulate values explicitly
and shape values that support business ideas. Such leaders avoid
using abstract terms, focusing instead on operational values that affect
business ideas. For example, GE's Jack Welch articulates the value of

"boundarylessness" in order to facilitate speed-to-market, the generation of ideas and the sharing of best practices. Andy Grove values constructive conflict because Intel's markets move too fast to waste time on wishy-washy feedback.

Emotional Energy

Winning leaders are motivated, and they motivate others regarding change and transition. Leaders must teach people how to energize others, both with face-to-face interactions and through large-scale organizational efforts.

Edge

Leadership is about making tough yes-no decisions. Winning leaders face reality and make decisions about people, products, businesses, customers and suppliers. They don't waffle. And they're willing to make decisions with imperfect data.

Business Stories

A leader engages other people by translating his or her points of view into a dynamic story. Based on these stories, people at all levels take actions that transform their organizations. Leaders' stories have these elements:

- A case for change
- An idea of where the organization is headed
- A perspective on how it will get there

Leadership Engine

This is a proven system for creating dynamic leaders at every level.

Winning companies are successful because they can adapt and capitalize on their unique circumstances — so no two are alike. Yet their Leadership Engines make them champions by developing — at all levels — leaders who have clear, teachable points of view that they use to run their businesses and teach others to be leaders.

The Leadership Engine:

Building Leaders at Every Level

Why do so many leadership programs produce so few lasting results?

Because they do not address the most critical component of leadership: the ability to teach others to be leaders.

It's possible for an organization to succeed for a while on the strength of one innovative product or a single dynamic leader. But to sustain that success, organizations constantly need to reinvent their products and themselves. And to do that, they need lots of leaders. They need leaders throughout the organization to make quick, smart decisions and get them implemented effectively today. And they need to teach new generations of leaders to do the same tomorrow.

The Leadership Engine Coaches' Clinic is a dynamic, hands-on program that not only hones the personal leadership abilities of the participants but also helps them teach others to do the same. Like an athletic camp, it pulls apart the game of leadership into its component parts, examines them and then brings them back together into a teachable point of view. And because it focuses on the real-life challenges that face the participants in their day-to-day work, it produces instant, valuable benefits for them and their organizations.

The Coaches' Clinic's approach is highly interactive. For each element of leadership, facilitators offer insights from *The Leadership Engine: How Winning Companies Build Leaders at Every Level* and benchmarks from world-class leaders. Then they challenge participants by asking, "What would you do about this?" In addition, all along the way, participants are encouraged to give tough, honest feedback to help each other improve.

The one-day Coaches' Clinic starts by asking participants to take a hard look at the business realities currently facing them. It then leads them to look at and to draw clear lessons from their own learning and experience, lessons that will help them improve their own leadership performance and the abilities of their employees. Participants will be led through the process of developing these lessons, or teachable points of view, in four critical leadership areas: Ideas, Values, Energy and Edge. Participants are asked to focus on:

Ideas

- Articulating the business ideas that have made their organization successful in the past
- Challenging their underlying assumptions
- Considering whether or not these ideas are sufficient to guarantee their organization's success in the future

Values

- Assessing their operating values to determine if their current values support or sabotage their business ideas
- Devising and discussing a plan for transforming the organization's values to support a change in strategy

Energy

- Examining the effects of positive and negative energy in an organization
- Generating positive energy and channeling stress-induced negative energy to positive uses

Edge

- Understanding the need for leaders to make tough, yes-no decisions based on the good of the organization
- Developing the needed skills for clearly and honestly facing both resource-allocation decisions and personnel decisions

The most important business investment you can make is developing more and better leaders throughout your organization. At the end of this one-day program, participants will have new leadership skills that they can apply in the workplace immediately. And they'll be committed teachers, dedicated to improving the abilities of others.

Just as you wouldn't want to make a bad investment in a plant, property or equipment, you shouldn't make one in leadership development either. *The Leadership Engine* Coaches' Clinic is based on reality and grounded in experience. Its methodology is proven. It delivers results.

For more information, please call Pritchett Rummler-Brache
at 1-800-992-5922

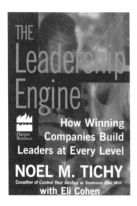

How Winning Companies Build Leaders at Every Level

NOEL M. TICHY
Coauthor of *Control Your Destiny or Someone Else Will*
with Eli Cohen

The Hardcover Book

The Leadership Engine: How Winning Companies
Build Leaders at Every Level
By Noel Tichy with Eli Cohen

Named one of the best business books of 1997

"I would be willing to wager that the companies in this book will be successful for a long time. This is because, as you will see, they have developed into organizations with a Leadership Engine — where leaders exist at all levels and leaders actively develop future generations of leaders. Once this engine gets running, it is hard for competitors to stop."

— Noel M. Tichy, author of *The Leadership Engine*

Why do some companies consistently win in the marketplace while others struggle from crisis to crisis? The answer, says Noel Tichy, is that winning companies possess a "Leadership Engine" — a proven system for creating dynamic leaders at every level.

Technologies, products and economies constantly change. To get ahead and stay ahead, companies need agile, flexible, innovative leaders who can anticipate change and turn on a dime to respond to new realities. Fortunately, says Tichy, just as everyone has untapped athletic potential, everyone has untapped leadership potential that can be developed. Winning leaders and winning organizations have figured out how to do it.

In this book, Tichy offers colorful and insightful best-practice examples from dozens of leaders, gathered from decades of research and practical experience.

• How does Jack Welch, for example, run the world's most valuable company — and spend 30 percent of his time on leadership development?

- How do the United States Navy SEALs and Army Rangers create leaders who can assume command of any team, anytime, anywhere?
- How did Ameritech break its hundred-year-old mentality of entitlement to create a culture where leaders develop other leaders?

Winning companies are successful because they can adapt and capitalize on their unique circumstances — so no two are alike. Yet their Leadership Engines make them champions by developing — at all levels — leaders who have clear, teachable points of view that they use to foster the abilities of others in four critical areas:

- Developing good business ideas
- Instilling values that support the successful implementation of those ideas
- Generating positive energy in themselves and others
- Making tough decisions

In his best-selling hardcover book, *The Leadership Engine*, Noel Tichy not only offers a major contribution to the understanding of how successful leadership works, but also provides concrete, proven methods for leaders developing leaders in any company or organization. As an added bonus, the section located at the end of the book provides hands-on development activities that you can use to improve your own leadership abilities and develop other leaders in your organization.

$19.95 plus shipping and handling

To order, please call Pritchett Rummler-Brache
at 1-800-992-5922

About the Authors

Noel Tichy

Noel Tichy is a professor at the University of Michigan Business School, where he specializes in leadership and organizational transformation. He has been a consultant to General Electric since 1982, including serving for two years as the head of GE's renowned Crotonville leadership development institute.

As a senior partner in Action Learning Associates, Tichy has consulted with clients around the world, including Royal Dutch/Shell, Coca-Cola, Ford, Ameritech, NEC and Royal Bank of Canada. His previous books include *Control Your Destiny or Someone Else Will* (co-authored with Stratford Sherman).

Eli Cohen

Eli Cohen is an independent researcher and consultant, and a partner in the firm Tichy Cohen Associates. He has consulted on strategy with a variety of clients while at Bain & Company. Prior to that he held operating positions at Procter & Gamble and Commerzbank AG.

Pritchett Rummler-Brache Consulting Services

Our consulting group has over two decades of experience working with organizations from all sectors to successfully plan and implement large-scale strategic change.

We'll help you:

- Design and implement a state-of-the-art merger integration strategy
- Address the people/organizational challenges associated with new information technology
- Radically redesign or make incremental improvements in your organization's key processes
- Develop or reconfigure your processes for effective e-commerce applications
- Address the organization design issues you face due to organizational growth and new business opportunities

If you would like to talk to one of our consultants about your unique change-related challenges, please call us at 1-800-992-5922.

Books by Pritchett Rummler-Brache

* *Managing Sideways: A Process-Driven Approach for Building the Corporate Energy Level and Becoming an "Alpha Company"*

* *New Work Habits for The Next Millennium:10 New Ground Rules for Job Success*

* *The Mars Pathfinder Approach to "Faster-Better-Cheaper": Hard Proof From the NASA/JPL Pathfinder Team on How Limitations Can Guide You to Breakthroughs*

* *Fast Growth: A Career Acceleration Strategy*

* *Outsourced: 12 New Rules for Running Your Career in an Interconnected World*

  MindShift: The Employee Handbook for Understanding the Changing World of Work

* *The Employee Handbook of New Work Habits for a Radically Changing World*

* *Firing Up Commitment During Organizational Change*

* *Business As UnUsual: The Handbook for Managing and Supervising Organizational Change*

* *The Employee Handbook for Organizational Change*

  Resistance: Moving Beyond the Barriers to Change

* *A Survival Guide to the Stress of Organizational Change*

* *High-Velocity Culture Change: A Handbook for Managers*

* *Culture Shift: The Employee Handbook for Changing Corporate Culture*

  The Ethics of Excellence

* *Service Excellence!*

  Teamwork: The Team Member Handbook

* *Team ReConstruction: Building a High Performance Work Group During Change*

* *Mergers: Growth in the Fast Lane*

  The Employee Guide to Mergers and Acquisitions

  After the Merger: Managing the Shockwaves

* *Making Mergers Work: A Guide to Managing Mergers and Acquisitions*

  Smart Moves: A Crash Course on Merger Integration Management

  The Quantum Leap Strategy

  you^2: A High-Velocity Formula for Multiplying Your Personal Effectiveness in Quantum Leaps

* *Leadership Engine: Building Leaders at Every Level,* based on Noel Tichy and Eli Cohen's best-selling hardcover from HarperBusiness, a division of HarperCollins Publishers.

ORDER FORM

The Leadership Engine:
Building Leaders at Every Level

**Please reference
customer number KA0106
when ordering**

A Rapid-Read Handbook

1-14 copies	____ copies at $9.95 each
15-29 copies	____ copies at $7.95 each
30-99 copies	____ copies at $5.95 each
100-999 copies	____ copies at $5.75 each
1,000-4,999 copies	____ copies at $5.50 each
5,000-9,999 copies	____ copies at $5.25 each
10,000 or more copies	____ copies at $5.00 each

Hardcover Book

Hardcover ____ copies at $19.95 each

Name _____

Job Title _____

Organization _____

Address _____

Country _____ Zip Code _____

Phone _____ Fax _____

Email _____

Purchase order number (if applicable) _____

*Applicable sales tax, shipping and handling charges
will be added. Prices subject to change.
Orders less than $250 require prepayment.
Orders of $250 or more may be invoiced.*

☐ Check Enclosed ☐ Please Invoice

☐ **VISA** ☐ **MasterCard** ☐ **AMERICAN EXPRESS**

Name on Card _____

Card Number _____ Expiration Date _____

Signature _____ Date _____

To order, call: 800-992-5922
fax: 972-731-1550
http://www.PritchettNet.com
or mail this form to the address below

PRITCHETT
RUMMLER-BRACHE
5800 Granite Parkway, Suite 450 • Plano, TX 75024
http://www.PritchettNet.com